WHO/RHB/95.1
Original: English
Distribution: General

DISABILITY PREVENTION AND REHABILITATION
IN PRIMARY HEALTH CARE

A guide for district health and rehabilitation managers

Rehabilitation
© World Health Organization
1995

CONTENTS

INTRODUCTION

This guide contains suggestions for action to strengthen disability prevention and rehabilitation within primary health care (PHC) services. It is addressed to rehabilitation and general health care personnel within the district health services, and particularly to the managers of those services, to promote collaboration.

The activities suggested here may take place within the context of a community-based rehabilitation (CBR) programme, but such a context is not required. If rehabilitation personnel are not routinely available, some of the activities could be undertaken by nurses within the district health services. It is preferable, however, for rehabilitation and general health care personnel to collaborate closely in this work. While physicians and nurses will be familiar with primary and secondary disability prevention, rehabilitation personnel will be more familiar with tertiary disability prevention. Physical and occupational therapists, as well as mid-level rehabilitation workers (MLRWs), can provide valuable input in some of the procedures used, for example, to prevent deformities or to train disabled people to move around or to take care of themselves.

The activities outlined in this guide are suggested for implementation at the district level. Their purpose is to

- assess the situation of disabled people in the district
- assess the district-level health services in the areas of disability prevention and rehabilitation
- set priorities for improving the situation
- make specific plans for action

The assessment and planning process need not be viewed as a burden on health care staff, but rather as a means to strengthen existing services so that they function more efficiently and effectively for all.

DEFINITIONS

The definition of the word *district* as used in this guide is taken from the *Manual of Epidemiology for District Health Management* (WHO 1989). The district is that most peripheral unit of local government and administration with comprehensive powers and responsibilities. It is the natural meeting point for "bottom-up" community planning and organization and "top-down" central government planning and development. The district is also the key level for the management of primary health care services. Since disability prevention and rehabilitation should be integrated into primary health care, the district plays a crucial role in strengthening these components of the health care services.

In addition to the district hospital, health facilities within the district health care system may include health posts, clinics, and health centres. The PHC workers include personnel who work in these facilities and also community health workers and traditional birth attendants, who may be volunteers.

The term *community-based rehabilitation (CBR)* as used in this guide is defined in *Community-Based Rehabilitation for and with People with Disabilities, A Joint Position Paper* by the International Labour Organization; the United Nations Educational, Scientific and Cultural Organization; and the World Health Organization (1994), as follows:

> Community-based rehabilitation is a strategy within community development for the rehabilitation, equalization of opportunities and social integration of all people with disabilities.
>
> CBR is implemented through the combined efforts of disabled people themselves, their families and communities, and the appropriate health, education, vocational and social services.

CBR activities at the community level rarely begin spontaneously. Rather, they are stimulated by contact from a ministry in charge of rehabilitation or by a nongovernmental organization (NGO). If a ministry is in charge of CBR, it is likely to be the one for health or social affairs. In either case, it is the responsibility of the Ministry of Health to provide disability prevention and medical rehabilitation services.

If the Ministry of Health (MOH) is responsible for the CBR programme, the community health worker may be asked to play an active role in disability prevention and rehabilitation. If another ministry is in charge and another volunteer, such as the community development worker, is the community contact for rehabilitation, the community health worker should also support the rehabilitation programme by promoting disability prevention and the social integration of disabled people. The manual *Training in the Community for People with Disabilities* (WHO 1989) contains information about the role of the community worker in a CBR programme, as well as information about what families can do to help someone with a disability.

Technical supervision for rehabilitation activities at the community level is provided by district-level health care staff. When the Ministry of Health is responsible for the CBR programme, the community workers report to staff in the nearest health care facility, which may be a health post or clinic. Rehabilitation referral services are also provided by rehabilitation staff at the district hospital. This may be a physical or occupational therapist, or a mid-level rehabilitation worker. Information about the management and support of rehabilitation services within the health care system can be found in *Community-based rehabilitation and the health care referral services—A guide for programme managers* (WHO/RHB/94.1).

The terms *impairment, disability,* and *handicap* as used in this guide are defined in the *International Classification of Impairments, Disabilities and Handicaps* (WHO 1980), as follows:

> Impairment, in the context of health experience, is any loss or abnormality of psychological, physiological or anatomical structure or function.

> Disability, in the context of health experience, is any restriction or lack (resulting from an impairment) of ability to perform an activity in the manner or within the range considered normal for a human being.

> Handicap, in the context of health experience, is a disadvantage for a given individual, resulting from an impairment or disability, that limits or prevents the fulfilment of a role that is normal (depending on age, sex, social and cultural factors) for that individual.

The following examples illustrate the application of these terms. Polio may result in paralysis of the leg muscles (impairment), which causes difficulty walking (disability). The person with difficulty walking may be denied a job because potential employers believe that someone with deformed legs is not intelligent (handicap). A caustic chemical substance splashed in the eyes of a child may result in scarred corneas (impairment), causing blindness (disability). The child may not be accepted into school because teachers do not know how to work with a blind child (handicap).

The terms *primary, secondary* and *tertiary prevention* of disabilities are defined as follows. Primary prevention consists of measures to prevent diseases, injuries, or conditions that can result in impairments or disabilities. Such measures include health education, immunization, maternal and child health services, and safety promotion. Together they comprise a major component of primary health care. District-level health care personnel are familiar with most primary prevention measures, although they may not have analyzed which of these are particularly important in disability prevention.

Secondary prevention consists of early intervention in the treatment of diseases, injuries, or conditions to prevent the development of impairments. Treatment of diseases (such as tuberculosis, onchocerciasis and diabetes) and injuries (such as burns or fractures) may prevent impairments and hence disabilities. Treatment of this type is usually initiated by the referral services, but follow-up is provided within the PHC system. As with primary prevention, the health care staff may not have analyzed which treatments are particularly related to disability prevention.

Tertiary prevention includes all measures to limit or reduce impairments or disabilities. It includes, for example, surgery to correct joint deformities and the provision of eye glasses for visual impairments or hearing aids for hearing impairments. In many instances, the treatment will reduce the impairment, as in the surgical correction of deformities. It may also reduce or even eliminate the disabilities that can result from impairments.

Tertiary prevention also includes the treatment of disabilities, or *rehabilitation.* Rehabilitation is the process whereby disability is minimized or eliminated. The rehabilitation process may include training in self-care, communication, or mobility. It may also include training to develop work skills.

CONTENT SUMMARY

This guide is intended to stimulate discussion and action to strengthen disability prevention and rehabilitation activities within the district-level health services. Discussion may be initiated by rehabilitation personnel, but the discussion process and any subsequent action will naturally involve the district health team and all district health care personnel.

Chapter 1 presents discussion guidelines for use by district health service staff to review the situation within the district relative to disability prevention and rehabilitation. The purpose of such discussion is to determine whether additional information is needed and to draft a schedule for further assessment and planning. The discussion material presented here is intended for use in a one-day workshop, involving staff from health facilities within the district. This group is referred to as the *district working group for disability prevention and rehabilitation (DPR).*

Chapter 2 contains guidelines for identifying existing information and for gathering additional information, as necessary. A research team could be formed for this purpose and the research carried out over an extended period, for example, six months.

Chapter 3 contains guidelines for assessment of the situation and planning of community-level activities. The guidelines provide for community involvement in this process and give examples of topics to be covered. A one-day workshop is proposed for this process.

Chapter 4 contains guidelines for assessment and planning by the district working group for disability prevention and rehabilitation (see Chapter 1). Based on the review findings and the plans prepared by the communities (see Chapter 3), the working group now prepares a plan to improve support to communities for rehabilitation activities and to strengthen district health services for disabled people. This planning process can be carried out during a one-day workshop or over several staff meetings.

Chapter 5 contains guidelines for review of the current system of monitoring and supervision within the district health care system to identify what components of disability prevention and rehabilitation are already included and to complement these, as necessary.

At the close of the review-assessment-planning process, the working group may present its findings and plans to an intersectoral group— involving all sectors having disability-related services at the district level— and propose collaboration to strengthen services for disabled people. **Chapter 6** presents suggested topics for discussion at such a meeting, for use in a one-day workshop.

CHAPTER 1.

LAUNCHING A DISTRICT INITIATIVE FOR DISABILITY PREVENTION AND REHABILITATION

DISABILITY ISSUES IN THE DISTRICT HEALTH SYSTEM

The role of the district health care system in primary and secondary prevention of disabilities is well-recognized. Its role in tertiary prevention, particularly rehabilitation, however, has yet to be established. In order to detect impairments and disabilities and to provide rehabilitation services to all disabled people within a district, it is necessary to draw upon the skills of a variety of health care personnel. Neither general health service staff nor rehabilitation staff alone can carry out all of the activities involved. Collaboration is needed.

Many developing countries do not offer rehabilitation services at the district level, but only at the national and provincial levels. Some countries may be able to post physical or occupational therapists to district hospitals. Others, however, do not have enough therapists for this purpose. In such cases, the district hospital may be staffed by mid-level rehabilitation workers (MLRWs), who receive shorter and more general training than therapists. Different countries have different titles for such workers, for example, rehabilitation technician or assistant.

Rehabilitation personnel at the district level seeking to strengthen their local disability prevention and rehabilitation services will, at some point, initiate discussions with the District Medical Officer (DMO) and the District Nursing Officer (DNO). If the DMO and the DNO agree that something should be done, then a process of discussion, planning, and action involving the district health team will follow. The suggestions presented here are intended as a guide in this process.

The specific points that are raised during initial discussions on this issue will vary, depending upon the local situation. The following are broad topics that may be covered:

- types of disabilities seen most frequently in the district
- causes of those disabilities
- measures currently taken to prevent those disabilities
- services provided by rehabilitation personnel at the district
  hospital

- services needed for disability prevention and rehabilitation, but not currently provided

If the district health team agrees that there is a need to improve services, a one-day workshop could then be held with representatives of primary health care workers within the district. These would include all nurses, but particularly nurses at the hospital; public health nurses; and psychiatric nurses working in community mental health. For the purposes of this guide, this group is referred to as the *district working group for disability prevention and rehabilitation (DPR)*.

TOPICS FOR DISCUSSION IN A ONE-DAY WORKSHOP

During the workshop, the DNO and a member of the district-level rehabilitation staff may begin by presenting a summary of their preliminary discussions, which would explain the purpose of the workshop and also serve as a basis for further discussion. At this point, it may be useful to raise the following broad questions:

- What is the current situation regarding disability prevention and rehabilitation activities in the district?

- Is there a need to strengthen existing services for disabled people?

- What are the resources available for this?

- What information is needed to clarify the situation, including needs and priorities?

Review of the current situation

In defining the current situation, the group could begin by reviewing types and causes of disabilities in the district; the conditions of disabled people and their families in their homes and communities; MOH guidelines for disability-related programmes; and types of services for disabled people provided by the MOH, other sectors, and NGOs.

All types of disabilities should be considered, for example difficulty moving, seeing, hearing, and learning, as well as behavioural difficulties, in both children and adults.

It may not be possible to identify causes of all of the disabilities known to the group. Nonetheless, as many causes should be identified as possible, including diseases, injuries, and congenital conditions. The most frequent causes and the preventable causes should be noted.

The situation of disabled people and their families should be described as thoroughly as possible, with reference to people with various types of disabilities and with disabilities of differing degrees of severity. The degree of their participation in daily activities, as appropriate, such as play, school, household work, community activities, and income generation, should be described. If their participation is limited, the reasons for this should also be described. An adult with a disability should be asked to participate in the discussion and to describe his or her experiences.

In discussing the situation of families of disabled people, the group members should describe which member of the family is usually responsible for the disabled person; what the family understands about the disability; what expectations they may have for the disabled person; and what needs they express or what services they request. Family members of disabled children should also participate in the discussions and describe their experiences.

Guidelines provided by the MOH for preventive, promotive, curative, or rehabilitative care should be reviewed to identify those specifically related to disabilities. The priorities of the MOH should also be identified and their relationship to disability prevention and rehabilitation noted. The strategies used by the MOH for delivery of services, e.g., institution-based, out-reach, and/or community-based, should also be analyzed.

The services specific to disability issues should be noted, together with the categories of health care personnel involved. If there are district services for disabled people that are provided by other ministries or by NGOs, these should also be noted. For example, appliances or special equipment needed by disabled people may be furnished by another ministry, an NGO, or the private sector. The proportion of disabled people with access to such services should be estimated as accurately as possible.

The general health services used by people with disabilities should be noted, e.g., whether disabled children benefit from routine services such as growth monitoring and immunizations, and whether disabled adults seek services for routine ailments as do other members of the community.

Determining the need to strengthen services

To determine whether there is a need to strengthen existing services, the working group should compare the current situation with what they feel should be done to provide disability prevention and rehabilitation.

Group members should examine each aspect of the current situation to decide whether it appears satisfactory or whether it should be improved.

At some point in this discussion, the group will find it useful to define realistically acceptable situations. They should try to avoid being too idealistic, but should also avoid focusing only on constraints to programme changes.

Determining the resources available

If as a result of these discussions, the group determines that there is a need to strengthen existing services, they must review what resources are available to do this. They should consider resources available within the community, the health care system, other ministries, NGOs, and the private sector.

Potential resources in the community include disabled people and their families; community leaders; organizations such as women's or youth groups; groups organized for economic purposes, such as income generating projects; and groups for health, community development, or other purposes, such as the Red Cross or Red Crescent.

The personnel and services available within the district health care system will have been identified earlier in the discussion. A list of potential resources, however, should also include referral services outside the district, at the provincial and national levels.

Resources within ministries other than the MOH would include personnel; equipment or facilities for education; and social services, vocational training, and employment services.

NGOs and the private sector may provide services for people with disabilities and may also be potential sources of funding.

Determining additional information needed

After reviewing the current situation, the group should list what additional information they require to clarify the situation. Such a list can be formulated by reviewing the notes of the discussion. Undoubtedly, the discussion covered points on which there were differing opinions. The health personnel, for example, may differ on what types of disabilities are most common in the district. Or there may be points raised for which the group has little or no information. For example, group members may not know what people with disabilities and their families would identify as priority needs. Additional information will clarify such points and help to round out the group's understanding of the current situation of disabled people in their district.

After determining what more they need to know, the group must decide how they will obtain it. There are a variety of information-gathering methods, for example, house-to-house surveys to identify disabled people, visits to the homes of disabled people to document their experiences and concerns, interviews with community leaders to identify community resources for the disabled, and interviews with representatives of other ministries and organizations involved in rehabilitation to identify resources available locally. The group may decide to use one or several of these.

After identifying methods for information gathering, the group members can select a research team, establish a broad time frame, and estimate a budget. The DMO and DNO may take responsibility for identifying the necessary resources, while the research group attends to information gathering.

The research team should include the DNO, a rehabilitation specialist, and personnel from the various district health services. The research team can now focus on the details of data collection.

CHAPTER 2.

INFORMATION GATHERING

The research team that is formed to develop methods for further information gathering will have several tasks:

- to identify and review existing sources of disability-related data
- to list what additional data must be gathered and from where
- to identify or develop tools for information gathering, for example, questionnaires
- to supervise the information gathering
- to prepare a summary of the current situation, based on the information gathered

REVIEW OF EXISTING INFORMATION

Existing sources of disability-related data may include health records; records and reports from a CBR programme; information about impairments identified in screening programmes; registries of disabled people; and disability-related information from a census or surveys.

None of the these information sources alone will present a complete picture of disability within the district. Information from a variety of sources, however, can be pieced together to provide a useful overview.

Health records

Records within the health care system may contain information relevant to disability prevention, i.e., data on diseases or conditions that can result in disabilities. Data may exist on the number of new cases of polio and measles each year, for example. However, there may be no record of the number or types of disabilities that have resulted from these. If there is a system for identifying and monitoring children at risk, based on assessment at birth or routine growth monitoring, those records could be used to identify children with possible impairments or disabilities.

The number of disabled people who seek health services or who are otherwise known to health care personnel may not be specified in routine health records, but this data could be obtained by the research team directly from health facility staff. Though incomplete, this information can add to what is known about age groups of disabled people and types of disabilities.

CBR records and reports

One of the routine activities of a CBR programme is the identification of disabled people. This is done by the community worker for rehabilitation, who also assesses each disabled person to determine what limitations the person has in daily activities and then to establish an appropriate training programme. If a CBR programme exists within the district, the research team should examine information from the communities in which it is active.

CBR records will provide information about types of disabilities, as well as demographic information, including the age, sex, and geographical location of disabled people. CBR records will also include data on the number of disabled children in local schools and the number of adults with income-producing work. The records, however, will not provide information about causes of disabilities.

Screening for impairments

Screening for impairments is usually carried out in a particular population, such as school children, or in a particular area, such as a part of the country where a potentially disabling condition occurs. The health or education services may carry out screening in the schools to identify visual or hearing impairments, for example, which can cause mild to moderate degrees of disability. The results of such screening may be available from the district office for education or for health.

Screening procedures usually identify impairments that do not cause severe disabilities, such as total blindness or deafness, or complete immobility. This is because screening is usually done in populations that are readily available, such as children in the schools. Children with severe disabilities are usually at home and not among the populations screened.

Registries

The MOH does not usually maintain a registry of disabled people. Such a registry is more likely to be found within a ministry that provides regular, long-term services or support to disabled people. If the ministry for social services or welfare is providing disability pensions, for example, the relevant office will have a list of pensioners. If a ministry is providing equipment, such as wheel chairs, it may maintain a list of recipients.

The research team should be aware of the shortcomings of registries. A registry usually contains a list of people who applied for a specific service, such as job placement or provision of special equipment. Such lists never include all people with disabilities in a particular area or with a specific type of disability. In addition, registries are usually not kept up to date, so they do not accurately reflect the ages and locations of disabled people.

Census or surveys

Countries are beginning to include disability-related questions in the census and routine surveys (health, demographic, and economic). This is now a recommended means of gathering disability-related data without incurring the cost of specific disability surveys. To determine if such data are available, the research team should contact the national statistical office.

The type of information obtained through the census or surveys will, of course, depend on the questions posed. The information usually consists of data on the number and types of disabilities or impairments, as well as standard demographic data. It may include data on education, marital, and employment status. From these, it may also be possible to extrapolate how many households include a disabled person.

ADDITIONAL INFORMATION TO BE SOUGHT

After examining all of the available data and in view of the information needs identified by the larger district working group, the research team now lists whatever information they feel is still required. At this point, to ensure that further information gathering does not duplicate similar efforts elsewhere in the country, the group should enquire with the national offices of the rehabilitation programme in the MOH and of the CBR programme, if that is in another ministry.

In any case, it is likely that more information will be needed on the personal experiences of disabled people and their families. District working group members may not agree on the real situation of disabled people. In order to strengthen disability prevention and rehabilitation services within their district, however, they must know exactly what needs of disabled people are not being met.

The working group may also want additional information about causes of disabilities. Local health records may not indicate causes of disabilities.

To plan an effective district disability prevention programme, however, it is necessary to know what diseases and injuries are common causes of disabilities in that district. Again, health care personnel may have varying opinions on this, which would indicate a need to verify conclusions with further data.

In addition, the health care personnel may be unaware of services for disabled people provided by other ministries, NGOs, or the private sector. This information is necessary, however, in order for them to make appropriate referrals—for disabled people to receive equipment, education, or training, for example—as part of the rehabilitation process.

The research team should list specific questions related to the above issues and to any other information still needed.

People to be interviewed

The information yet to be gathered will determine the groups of people to be interviewed. It is likely that these groups will include

- disabled people
- family members of disabled people
- community leaders
- representatives of community organizations
- representatives of other sectors involved in rehabilitation

TOOLS FOR INFORMATION GATHERING

If the research team decides that it is necessary to carry out a house-to-house survey in selected communities to identify disabled people, there may be tools already available for this purpose. If screening is to be done, for example, to detect delayed development among children brought to health centres for growth monitoring, standard milestones of child development can be used.

If the research team plans to undertake house-to-house surveys to determine the needs and priorities of disabled people and their families, they will first need to prepare a questionnaire. A questionnaire will also be needed to gather information from personnel in other sectors of rehabilitation services. The following guidelines can be used in formulating questions:

- Questions should be as brief as possible.
- Each question should cover only one issue.

- Questions should be phrased in the language and style of the people interviewed. Their level of education and background must be considered. For example, medical terms should not be used in questions intended for people outside the health care system.

- A combination of closed- and open-ended questions should be used. Closed-ended questions give respondents a selection of answers from which to choose. The choice may be simply "yes" or "no," or the answers may be presented in a list from which the respondent selects one or more. Open-ended questions leave the answers entirely to the respondent.

  Respondents generally feel more comfortable with closed- rather than open-ended questions. Closed-ended questions are also easier to analyze because of the limited number of responses.

  A disadvantage of closed-ended questions is that the answers provided may not include the answers the respondent would like to give.

  An advantage of open-ended questions is that they allow original answers—including those the interviewer may not anticipate.

  A disadvantage of open-ended questions is that the resulting data may be difficult to analyze because of the variety of responses. Too many open-ended questions may also make interviewees uncomfortable; they may want to give the "right" answers, and the questions offer them no guide.

  Interviewees may, however, appreciate one or two open-ended questions that allow them to express their opinions freely. For this reason, effective questionnaires often use mostly closed-ended questions, with one or two open-ended questions at the end.

After the questions are formulated for the group(s) of people to be interviewed, they should be tested for clarity. The testing is done by means of sample interviews. Questions meant for disabled people, for example, are tested by doing sample interviews with disabled people.

A final review of the questions should be made to verify that each one provides information that is needed and that can actually be obtained. The research team should remember: *Information that will not be used should not be gathered.*

SUPERVISION OF INFORMATION GATHERING

The research team should prepare guidelines for the interviewers on how to explain the purpose of the interview, how to pose the questions, and how to record the responses. Before interviews are conducted, all of the interviewers should meet to review the guidelines and ensure uniformity in their approach.

Communities selected for household interviews should be representative of social and economic conditions within the district. For the convenience of the staff who will supervise the operation, it may be desirable to gather information close to the district hospital. This sector, however, may not be typical of general conditions throughout the district. If necessary, arrangements should be made to train staff or community health workers in other parts of the district to carry out the interviews. Community health workers would be a logical choice for carrying out household interviews. Members of the research team could then focus on interviews with personnel of various sectors and services.

If a CBR programme is established and information is available from the areas covered by the programme, the research team must decide whether to seek further information in those areas or whether data is more needed from other parts of the district. The working group should remember that when disabled people or their families are interviewed about their problems, they will rightfully expect something to be done to address those problems. Interviews should therefore be conducted in areas where follow-up services can be provided immediately.

In preparation for household interviews, the interviewers should first contact the community leaders of the selected communities and explain the purpose of the interviews. The interviewers should also first contact organizations of disabled people to see if they have representatives at the district or community levels who could help identify disabled people. If not, disabled people in the community can be identified through community leaders. For interviews with personnel in various services, the interviewers should first contact the directors of the services. They should also inform the heads of organizations from whom information will be sought.

After appropriate preparation, the information gathering should be carried out. Based on the scope of the surveys and the number of personnel available to do the work, a specific time frame should be established for the process.

SUMMARY OF THE CURRENT SITUATION

After the data has been analyzed and the resulting information combined with what was already known, the research team can now prepare a summary of the situation to serve as a basis for assessment and planning at the community level.

A major component of the summary will be about the disabled people. This data may come from surveys, screenings, registries, and records from disability-related services, including CBR programme records.

**Examples of data
gathered from existing sources**

- number of disabled people according to type of disability, sex, and age group (0-4, 5-14, 15-49, 50, and over)
- number of people receiving services,e.g.,
    - training to increase function in daily activities
    - counselling for disabled person and/or family
    - provision of equipment or appliances
    - assistance to enter local school
    - assistance to develop work skills
    - assistance to person or family, e.g., youth group responsible for taking a disabled child to school, a woman's group providing a caregiver for disabled person two afternoons a month

---

Additional information about the situation of disabled people may have been obtained from interviews with disabled people and their families. If

---

Examples of information obtained from interviews

- number of communities and household visited
- number of people interviewed, i.e., disabled people and/or family members
- number of disabled people who require the assistance of a family member for daily activities
- causes of disabilities described by disabled people and/or their families
- expectations about the future of the disabled person, as described by the person and/or the family
- socio-economic condition of disabled people and/or their families
- problems or needs identified by disabled people and/or their families

---

a CBR programme is established in the district, interviews may have been done in communities with and without CBR programmes. If so, a comparison can be made of the two situations.

Using the data gathered, the district working group for DPR can now prepare a brief description of the disability prevention and rehabilitation services within their district. If interviews were conducted with personnel in the health services, a summary of this information should also be presented. The summary may include information about health service activities during a specific period of time, such as the past year.

Examples of information obtained from the health services

- the number of disabled people who come to the clinics or health centres for general health care
- the number and types of disabilities identified by health service personnel
- the types and numbers of services provided to disabled people

Information about services provided by other sectors and NGOs may also be summarized.

CHAPTER 3.

ASSESSMENT AND PLANNING WITH THE COMMUNITY

Assessment and planning should start with the community, where the rehabilitation of disabled people actually takes place. If there is a CBR programme in the district, at least some of the communities will be aware of disability-related issues. If there is no CBR programme in the district, the health personnel and community leaders should carry out awareness-raising prior to the workshop. If this has not been done, the workshop may have to focus on awareness-raising and a second workshop planned to analyze the situation, identify priorities, and draw up a plan of action.

COMMUNITY ASSESSMENT

The group that meets for assessment and planning at the community level should include the DNO, rehabilitation personnel, representatives of the district working group for DPR, representatives from the communities where research has been conducted, representatives from communities with CBR (if they were not included in the research), and representatives of disabled people and their families. This group is referred to here as the *community working group for DPR.*

The discussions of this group should focus on the situation of people with disabilities and what can be done to prevent disabilities and promote rehabilitation in the community. However, the need for support from the referral services may also be addressed. The group should aim to review

---

**Examples of issues of particular interest
at the community level**

- causes of disabilities
- age groups of disabled people
- family situations of disabled people
- educational opportunities for disabled children
- ability of disabled adults to contribute to the support of their families

---

the information available on the situation of disabled people in the community, establish priorities in reference to this information, and then draw up a plan of action.

Table 1 on page 17 gives examples of how two factors—the situation of disabled people and the current services or actions that address them—might be compared. The table also gives examples of possible actions to be taken. The community working group should be prepared to analyze various aspects of the situation of disabled people, in each case trying to determine if action is needed and, if so, what it should be.

COMMUNITY PLANNING

Setting priorities

Once the community working group has analyzed the situation, it should be clear what actions are needed. The group will then need to set priorities for action. To do this, they will need to establish criteria for setting priorities. Example of such criteria are as follows:

- the action addresses a problem or need identified by disabled people and/or their families

- the action can be carried out with the present resources or resources that can be obtained

There may be other criteria, depending upon the situation. For example, if the data reviewed show more disabilities among children of school age than in other age groups, then actions to benefit these children may be a priority. If there is a major cause of disabilities in some communities, the reduction of disabilities as the result of that cause may be a priority.

There may be different criteria and different priorities among the communities in the district. During their discussions, the working group

---

Examples of priorities

- to change attitudes in the community toward disabled people with disabilities

- to integrate disabled adults into community activities

- to provide assistance to families with disabled persons who require daily care

---

16

Table 1

Example of an analysis of a community situation

Situation of people with disabilities	Current action (or lack of action) to address the situation	Community and district actions that could be taken
People believe that disabilities are the result of wrong-doing	No public education is available on causes of disabilities	Provide education to the community and counselling to families of disabled people
Disabilities in children are not identified until they are two to three years old	Screening for disabilities is not provided for infants and young children	Incorporate screening for disabilities into growth monitoring programme(s)
Families do not know what to expect for their disabled children	Information and counselling is not routinely provided	Provide counselling to disabled people and/or their families
Most disabilities in young adults are caused by accidents	Health education is available about accidents in the home, but not about accidents involving the road, leisure activities, or work	Provide health education on all types of accidents and assist local youth groups to address the issue
Most disabled children do not attend school	Local schools accommodate only children who have no disabilities or who have mild to moderate difficulty walking	Facilitate acceptance of disabled children by local schools
Most disabled adults do not have income-producing work	Disabled adults lack opportunities to learn income-producing skills	Explore community resources for income-generation (before looking outside the community)

can note both common and unique priorities. Each priority identified may require numerous actions in order to impact the situation. To be realistic, therefore, each community may decide to initially set only two or three priorities.

When setting priorities, the group should consider the resources that will be needed to carry out the actions implied. They should note available resources and also any resources that are lacking. The group should be realistic about resources that can actually be obtained.

A major resource available in the community is people. Community and religious leaders, members of community committees and organizations, people concerned about their friends or neighbours with disabilities, and disabled people themselves can all participate in improving the situation of disabled people. In addition, some members of the community will possess knowledge and skills—for income generation, for example—that they can pass on to disabled people.

One resource that should be easy to obtain from outside the community is information. If there is a need to educate communities about the causes of disabilities, for example, staff from the health services can provide information to the community through presentations and the distribution of written material. Health service personnel, such as health educators, can help to develop educational messages for distribution on posters, in flyers and newspapers, or on the radio. If there is a need to promote a better understanding of the potential abilities of disabled people, representatives from the rehabilitation referral services and disabled people themselves can help here.

Some resources may take time to obtain. For example, if a community in the district wants to develop a CBR programme, it will take time to organize a training programme for community workers. There may also be constraints that limit expansion of the CBR programme, for example, if there are not enough rehabilitation personnel to staff the district hospital.

After considering the priorities for action and the resources available, the community working group can propose a plan of action for the community.

Plan of action

The plan of action states what goals are to be achieved within a given time period, what actions will be carried out to achieve the goals, and what indicators will be used to determine that the goals have been achieved. The goals specify what changes should occur in the situation of people with disabilities and are followed by a list of the actions needed to reach

the goals. As noted above, each community should limit itself to only two
or three goals since each of them will require a variety of actions.

The period of time needed to achieve the goals will vary according the
actions to be taken. The group should note, however, that to change any
particular aspect of the situation of disabled people will probably take a
minimum of one year. This is because most changes in social behaviour
involve a change in people's attitudes, which requires a change in their
understanding of the situation. To provide education and to stimulate such
a change take time.

The plan of action should include indicators for each goal to determine
when the goal has been achieved. For example, if a goal is to have adults
with disabilities acquire income-producing skills, the indicator may be the
percentage of disabled adults in the community expected to have income-
producing work within a given period of time. It is not realistic to expect
that every disabled adult will attain the goal. Some may not want to work,
or some may have disabilities that prevent them from working.

The boxes below and on page 20 present two examples of goals, with the
actions to be taken to achieve them, time frames, and indicators.

Plan of action for the community

First example of a goal, actions, time frame, and indicator

Goal	Community members will have a better understanding of the causes of disabilities.*
Actions	Information will be prepared and given to all local organizations for presentation and distribution to members.
	Posters providing information about the most common causes of disability will be placed in public locations.
	Community leaders will support the education campaign and will discourage traditional beliefs that result in the rejection of disabled people.
Time frame	One year
Indicator	The majority of people interviewed regarding causes of disabilities will know common causes in the community.**

* The initial review of the local situation indicated that community members did not
know the causes of disabilities and held the traditional belief that disabilities were
the result of wrong-doing.

** To be determined by random interviews at the end of one year.

> **Plan of action for the community**
>
> **Second example of a goal, actions, time frame, and indicator**
>
> **Goal** Children with mild to moderate disabilities will be included in local school classes.
>
> **Actions** Discussions will be held with families of disabled children of school age to clarify the needs of their children, e.g., for transportation to and from school, assistance moving around the school building, special seating in the classroom, or other assistance, as appropriate.
>
> Discussions will be held with the District Education Officer regarding the necessary actions to take to include disabled children in local schools.
>
> Discussions will be held with the head teacher of each local school to gain his or her cooperation for including disabled children in school classes.
>
> Discussions will be held with the teachers who will have students with special needs in their classrooms.
>
> Organizations in the community will be asked for volunteers to assist teachers in working with children having special needs.
>
> **Time frame** One year
>
> **Indicator** Children with mild to moderate disabilities will be included in local school classes.

After the action plans have been drafted, the community representatives must return to their individual communities with the proposed plans. The community may want to modify the plan, of course, but since the plan is solidly based on an analysis of the situation and the identification of realistic priorities and resources, it is unlikely that significant changes will be made.

The accomplishments of the community working group for DPR in identifying needs, priorities, and goals for the community has now provided a basis for a similar process to be undertaken by the district working group for DPR.

CHAPTER 4.

ASSESSMENT AND PLANNING FOR THE DISTRICT HEALTH SERVICES

Following the assessment and planning with the community, the district working group meets again to carry out a similar process for the district health services. This can be done in a one-day workshop or over several staff meetings.

HEALTH SERVICE ASSESSMENT

Assessment and planning for strengthening disability prevention and rehabilitation within the district health services should be based on 1) the analysis of the situation in the district and 2) the priorities set by the communities.

A great deal of work in these two areas will have already been done by the district and community working groups, yet the health service personnel may still have concerns that have not been addressed.

Examples of concerns of the health care staff

- types of impairments and disabilities identified
- specific causes of disabilities
- number of disabled people identified
- social and economic situation of disabled people and/or their families
- number of disabled people who have received services from the MOH in the past year
- types of services provided
- preparedness of health care staff to address disability-related issues
- possible need for additional MOH guidelines for disability prevention and rehabilitation

---

The assessment and planning process of the district working group will naturally focus on the particular concerns of the health services. To ensure that the health care services respond to community needs, the priorities and goals set by the community working group should also be addressed as part of the district planning process.

The research team that prepared for the community planning and assessment process can also prepare for the district planning and assessment process. They should gather any additional information needed, such as specific data from the health services, e.g., the number of disabled people treated by the health services in the past year.

Using all of the information available, the district working group now analyzes the response of the health services to the situation of disabled people to determine whether the response is adequate. If they feel it is not, a plan of action should be made to strengthen services.

In reviewing the situation, the group should analyze what could have been done to prevent disabilities, to detect the disabilities earlier, or to provide interventions to limit the impact of the disabilities. The group should also invite disabled people and their family members to discuss these issues.

The analysis of the health services will be more detailed than the community analysis with reference to the types and causes of disabilities, the situation of disabled people, and the disability prevention and rehabilitation activities already undertaken by the health services. The box below and the boxes on pages 23 and 24 give examples of questions that may be raised with regard to these factors.

**Examples of questions about types and causes
of impairments and disabilities**

- what are the most common types of impairments and disabilities?

- in which age groups are disabilities most common?

- which causes of impairments and disabilities are preventable?

- what are the health services doing to prevent disabilities?

- what more could be done by the health services directly or by other sectors to promote disability prevention?

- do the communities have action plans related to the causes of disabilities, e.g., for community education programmes?

- what can the health services do to support the community actions?

**Examples of questions about the situation
of people with disabilities**

- what is the socio-economic status of disabled people and/or their families, and what is the distribution of disabled people by socio-economic group?

- which family member is usually responsible for the disabled person?

- how well do disabled people and/or their families understand their disabilities—cause, prognosis, limitations, possible progression?

- how do disabled people and/or their families react to the disability, e.g., with acceptance, anger, guilt, shame, resignation?

- how does the community react to disabled people and/or their families, e.g., with pity, support, rejection?

- how can the health services address these issues?

- do the communities have action plans related to these issues?

- how can the health services support the community actions?

**Examples of questions about health care services
for people with disabilities**

- what percentage of disabled people identified seek health services?

- what are their disabilities?

- what services do they seek—for general health problems or for assistance related to their disabilities?

- what services are provided?

- how many disabled people were initially identified by the health services?

- what are the reasons why disabled people do not seek health care services, e.g., lack of awareness about what is available, lack of expectations, or inability to benefit from the services currently offered?

- what more could be done by the health services?

- do the communities have action plans related to these issues?

- how can the health services support the community actions?

Table 2 on page 25 presents examples of several issues that could be addressed as part of the analytical process. This example follows the pattern of comparison used for the community analysis (see Table 1 on page 17) in which two factors—the situation of disabled people and current actions relevant to the situation—are noted, followed by actions suggested to improve the situation.

HEALTH SERVICE PLANNING

Setting priorities

At this point, the working group will have clarified what actions could be taken to strengthen disability prevention and rehabilitation services throughout the district. Indeed, workshop discussions may have identified many needs and ideas for action. Because resources are limited, however, priorities will need to be set for district-level health activities, just as they were for the community action.

The criteria for setting the priorities for the health services may be the same as those for the community, for example:

• the action addresses a problem or need identified by disabled people or their families

• the action can be carried out with present resources or resources that can be obtained

Table 2

Example of an analysis of the district health services

Situation of people with disabilities	Current action (or lack of action) to address the situation	District health service actions that could be taken
The number of children with limited mobility due to burn scars is greater than the number previously known to the health services	No specific action	Conduct a health education programme for the prevention of burns; carry out home visits to advise the families of children with burn scars on how to care for the scars and how to maintain mobility in the affected limb(s)
Children with all types of disabilities are rarely brought to the health centres for growth monitoring or for treatment of common childhood illnesses	No specific action	Carry out home visits to families of disabled children to assess their general health and development; encourage family members to bring the children for care when needed and to promote the most normal development possible for the child
Adults with disabilities who were hospitalized at the onset of their disabilities have not received follow up in the community	No specific action	Carry out home visits to determine who should receive follow up for prevention of deformities or for functional training; improve communication and referral between PHC and hospital staff

Alternatively, the health services may select other criteria, such as:

- the action will decrease or eliminate the most common causes of disability in the district

- the action will benefit the majority of disabled people in the district

Each priority identified may imply a number of actions, so the health services, like the communities, will want to limit their priorities, although these may be reviewed and revised periodically.

In determining priorities, the group must of course consider the resources available and the possibility of obtaining additional resources.

A major resource for the health services is people, i.e., the staff of the various health facilities. It may be possible to significantly increase disability-related work simply by creating awareness among the staff. It is important, though, that rehabilitation services not become a burden. Rehabilitation services should be considered part of the routine work of the health care personnel. The goal of primary health care is to provide health for all, and, this obviously includes people with disabilities.

In addition to creating awareness among staff, it may be necessary to provide in-service training in certain aspects of disability prevention or rehabilitation. It may be possible to include this in the regular in-service training programme, or it may be necessary to identify funds specifically for rehabilitation training.

After considering programme priorities in relation to resources, the working group can now prepare a plan of action.

Plan of action

The health service personnel should use the same process for developing a plan of action as was used to develop the community plans, which is to

- state goals specifying what changes should occur in the situation of disabled people

- list the actions to be carried out to meet the goals

- indicate the time frame for meeting the goals

- identify indicators to show to what degree the goals have been achieved

An example of a plan of action with a goal, actions to be taken, a time frame, and an indicator is presented in the box on page 27.

Plan of action for the district health services

Example of a goal, time frame, and indicator

Goal	In designated communities, each family with a disabled child between the ages of 0 and 5 will know how to prevent deformities and/or how to promote the most normal development possible for the child.
Actions	Identify all of the disabled children in the designated communities [if this has not been done previously] by means of house-to-house visits by the community health workers (CHWs). Train CHWs, as necessary. Ask each family to bring the child to the nearest health facility; visit the homes of those who do not comply. Assess each child and establish a record of each child's disability and developmental status. Counsel family members regarding 1) the prevention of deformities, 2) the need to stimulate the child's development through communication, movement, and play, and 3) family problems that can result from the occurrence of a disability. Meet with families and children periodically to provide supervision and encouragement and to monitor the children's development.
Time frame	One year
Indicator	At least one family member of each child will be able to demonstrate appropriate activities for prevention of deformities and stimulation of development in the child.

Each goal set for the health care services may require the implementation of many activities. Therefore, like the communities, the health care staff may decide to set only two or three goals.

This work being done by the district working group forms the basis for the establishment of a system for monitoring and supervision of disability prevention and rehabilitation activities within the district. The district working group may ask the research team to identify what changes are needed in the current system to ensure that the expanded activities will also be monitored and supervised.

CHAPTER 5.

MONITORING AND SUPERVISION FOR DISABILITY PREVENTION AND REHABILITATION

Monitoring and supervision are ongoing processes that provide programme managers with information about actions being taken by the programme staff and the result of those actions. The managers compare the information they receive with the programme objectives and planned activities. Based on that comparison, managers give feedback to the staff and specify any changes needed to meet programme objectives.

The monitoring and supervision of disability prevention and rehabilitation activities should be an integral part of routine monitoring and supervision carried out within the district health services. The research team can review the current routine and make recommendations to the district health team regarding necessary changes. The district health team, and particularly the district medical officer, can discuss the recommendations with the research team and then decide what changes will be made so that disability prevention and rehabilitation activities are included in the system for monitoring and supervision.

WHAT TO MONITOR

To determine whether the current system for monitoring adequately covers disability prevention and rehabilitation activities, the research team will need to identify what activities are currently monitored, what activities should be monitored, and what procedures should be added to the monitoring process.

The action plans developed by the district working group for DPR will help to determine what information is needed for monitoring. The example of a goal and indicator given on page 30 is from the plan of action presented in the box on page 27.

In order to monitor progress towards this goal, the indicator should be incorporated into routine monitoring procedures. If the health service has limited its number of goals, and thus indicators, as suggested in Chapter 4, then it may not be difficult to incorporate a few additional indicators into the current district monitoring process.

<table>
<tr><td>Goal</td><td>In designated communities, each family with a disabled child between the ages of 0 and 5 will know how to prevent deformities and/or how to promote the most normal development possible for the child.</td></tr>
<tr><td>Indicator</td><td>At least one family member of each child will be able to demonstrate appropriate activities for prevention of deformities and stimulation of development in the child.</td></tr>
</table>

REVIEW OF THE CURRENT SYSTEM

Although monitoring and supervisory processes are closely related, they can be analyzed separately to determine whether the established routines are adequate to cover activities related to disability prevention and rehabilitation.

Monitoring

To review the current monitoring process, the research group analyzes the current system of records and reporting to identify information relevant to disability issues. The following questions may be useful in guiding the review process:

- What data are currently reported to the district level by the peripheral services, and what portion of this data relates to disability prevention and rehabilitation?

  Data on mortality, immunization coverage, and communicable diseases are commonly reported, but some countries or regions within countries may have additional reporting requirements.

- What activities of the health service staff are reported?

- Is other information reported that is used to monitor the impact of the health services?

- If there is a CBR programme in the district, what information is available from the CBR programme records?

  The following records may be maintained by the community rehabilitation worker:

  - number of people with disabilities

  - baseline information on the functional limitations of disabled people participating in the programme

- number of people who improved in their function in daily activities and/or are able to participate in school, work, or social activities

- number of referrals, with reference to type of service or equipment provided

- number of disabled children who have entered school as a result of the CBR programme

- number of disabled adults who have undergone skills training or who have income-producing work as a result of the CBR programme

If such information is already available and regularly reported to the district-level supervisor of the CBR programme, it is not necessary for the general health services to record and report the same information.

A review of the monitoring process for the health services may show that some information related to the prevention of diseases or conditions that can cause disabilities is covered, but that there is no routine reporting of information directly related to disabled people or rehabilitation.

Supervision

Supervision of the health services from the district level is generally carried out in several ways, such as through review of reports, staff meetings, and on-site visits to peripheral health facilities.

A review of the routine supervision of health care activities will indicate whether supervision covers activities related to disability prevention and rehabilitation. Two aspects of the staff's responsibilities should be given particular attention: 1) work related to early detection of disabilities and 2) the provision of counselling to disabled people and/or their families.

If regular health services do not include assessment of children for early detection of disabilities, then supervisory responsibilities will not cover this area. If this proves to be the case, measures to detect disabilities can be incorporated into routine growth monitoring programmes and supervisory responsibilities expanded accordingly.

If nurses have not previously been expected to provide advice or counselling to disabled people and/or their families, there may be no specific reference to this in routine supervisory procedures. It is generally expected, however, that nurses will provide advice and counselling to help people protect or improve their health, and since disabled people are members of the community, they have a right to such advice and counselling. Hence this is not an additional task for the staff, but rather one aspect of their regular responsibilities.

If there is a CBR programme within the district health care services, there may be a special arrangement for the supervision and support of community health workers who undertake rehabilitation activities. The CHWs usually report to the nurses at the nearest health facility, who provide them guidance and support in their primary health care work. The nurses should also provide guidance and support for the CHWs in their rehabilitation work. In addition, the CHWs may receive technical support from the mid-level rehabilitation worker (MLRW) at the district hospital.

Technical input from the MLRW to the CHW will vary, depending on the number of MLRWs at the district hospital and the availability of transport for on-site visits. If a MLRW is able to travel regularly throughout the district, the technical support to the CHW will be greater than if the MLRW communicates with the CHW only in regard to referrals to the hospital. If the MLRW does not visit the community, there will be more referrals to the hospital, but the support from the MLRW will still be limited. When the MLRW is unable to visit the community, the CHWs will need greater support from the nurses. The MLRW will probably have to provide in-service training for the nurses to help them feel confident with this responsibility.

ADDITIONAL NEEDS FOR MONITORING AND SUPERVISION

A review of the monitoring and supervisory procedures of the health care services may show a need to modify the current system to improve coverage of disability prevention and rehabilitation activities. The boxes on the following pages present examples of areas that could be monitored and suggestions on how the monitoring could be done.

If monitoring procedures are modified, then supervisory procedures must also be modified accordingly. If monitoring procedures are broadened to include the areas presented in the boxes above, for example, then supervisory procedures must be expanded to ensure that the staff is properly trained to

- identify types and causes of disabilities or make appropriate referrals

- carry out procedures for detecting disabilities

- provide advice and counselling on the prevention of deformities and the stimulation of normal development in children with different types of disabilities

Example

What to monitor

Incidence, prevalence, and causes of disabilities

How to monitor

Each of the most peripheral health centres maintains a registry of disabled people in their communities, recording for each individual the type of disability, the cause, the age of the person, and the age at the onset of the disability.

An annual summary of the information is submitted to the district level, which then compiles data on

- the number of new disabilities that began during the year reported (incidence)
- the total number of people with disabilities—new and old (prevalence)
- the types of disabilities and their causes

Example

What to monitor

Early detection of disabilities in children ages 0-5

How to monitor

One method is to monitor only children considered to be at risk of disability. These would be children who have had a serious illness, such as meningitis, malaria, or any condition causing a high fever, convulsions, or unconsciousness for more than one day; or children who do not develop as other children their age. The health cards of these children should be marked with coloured stickers to identify them for special attention when they are brought to the health services for routine growth monitoring and immunization.

Another method is to monitor all children through routine assessments of vision, hearing, and developmental milestones. This could be done approximately every six months for the first two years, and then annually for three years. The assessment could be incorporated into routine growth monitoring.

Example

What to monitor

Number of mothers of disabled children age 0-5 who are able to promote the most normal development possible for their children

How to monitor

Each peripheral health centre maintains a list of the mothers (or other family members) who have received advice and counselling on the prevention of deformities and stimulation of development appropriate for their disabled children.

When a mother (or other family member) of one of the children is able to demonstrate all of the activities advised by the health care staff, this is recorded by the staff.

After the research team prepares its recommendations, the team will consult with the district working group before presenting the recommendations to the district health team (DHT). Once agreed by the district working group, the final recommendations can be presented to the DHT, who will decide on procedures for monitoring and supervising the implementation of the action plans.

The district working group, in collaboration with the DHT, may also wish to present the action plans to other sectors working in rehabilitation. This could form a basis for collaboration and for developing or strengthening a comprehensive rehabilitation programme within the district.

CHAPTER 6.

INTERSECTORAL COLLABORATION FOR DISABILITY ISSUES

People with disabilities benefit greatly from coordinated rehabilitation services. If one service, such as health, is aware of what is offered by another service, such as education or social affairs, the health service can inform disabled people of this and also make appropriate referrals. The degree of coordination among rehabilitaion services varies from country to country, but can also vary from district to district within a country.

If there is a CBR programme in the district, disability issues may already be a subject for discussion at district-level intersectoral meetings. A District Development Committee (DDC), for example, may be a focal point for addressing the issues. If this is the case, a representative from the health sector may have already reported on its activities to strengthen disability prevention and rehabilitation.

If disability issues have not been discussed at district-level intersectoral meetings, the district working group can propose that this be initiated. The representative of the health services to the DDC can inform other members of the DDC about the health sector initative and propose a meeting of representatives from relevant sectors and concerned NGOs to discuss the strengthening of all rehabilitation services. The relevant sectors may include education, social affairs, labour/employment, and local government. The concerned NGOs would include those of disabled people, as well as organizations for disabled people and organizations providing special services that contribute to rehabilitation.

INTERSECTORAL DISCUSSIONS

A one-day workshop could then be held for representatives from interested parties, with the following items on the agenda:

- presentation of the findings of the health sector review of the situation of disabled people and the health care services

- presentation of the rehabilitation activities of other ministries and organizations

- presentation of the plans of the health sector to strengthen services for disability prevention and rehabilitation

- discussion to identify ways to strengthen collaboration among all
  sectors

The workshop would not be a forum in which each sector decides whether
it would also like to review its activities and develop a plan to strengthen
its services. That would have to be done within each sector.

During the workshop, other sectors and organizations may have the
opportunity to describe their current or planned activities. The box below
contains examples of activities related to rehabilitation that may be in
progress in various sectors and organizations. These may also be

Examples of activities of sectors (other than health) and organizations relevant to disability issues

Education	Provide advice on special education to teachers in local schools with disabled students Provide a special education teacher to visit local schools to assess disabled children
Social services	Provide disability pensions Provide appliances or equipment for disabled people
Labour or employment	Provide vocational training for disabled people Assist in job placement for disabled people
Local government	Ensure that disability issues are considered in discussions of community development
Organizations for disabled people	Promote skills training and job placement Promote integration of people with disabilities in programmes for people without disabilities Promote activities to raise awareness of disability issues
NGOs, such as women's and youth groups, Red Cross or Red Crescent	Assist disabled individuals and/ or their families Promote necessary changes in beliefs and attitudes related to disability Ensure that disabled people become active members of the organizations

activities not yet initiated, but which could be undertaken as part of a collaborative effort to strengthen services and opportunities for disabled people.

Some of the activities listed, such as the advice on special education or special skills training, require specific expertise. Other activities, such as awareness raising and promotion of social integration of people with disabilities, could be done by several ministries and organizations. These may be activities that could be proposed for joint efforts.

The immediate outcome of the workshop may be to establish a schedule for regular intersectoral (including ministries and NGOs) discussions on disability issues. The need for such discussions will depend on what is already being done about disability issues at the district level. As noted above, there may be a district committee that addresses disability issues. If that is the case, the representatives from the various sectors of rehabilitation must decide if there is a need for them to meet separately to discuss their own activities in depth and to strengthen their collaboration. The group may decide that such discussions are necessary, at least for a limited time, to strengthen communication and collaboration.

The initial goals of intersectoral discussions may be to

- present reports of the developments in various sectors
- strengthen collaboration for referrals
- clarify what activities might be carried out jointly

The group may decide to set goals for what should be achieved through the discussions and also to identify indicators for these goals. For example, if a goal is to increase referrals of disabled people, an indicator of success would be an increased number of referrals. However, care must be taken to ensure that the referrals are appropriate and necessary.

CONCLUSION

This guide has provided suggestions for steps that can be taken within the health care sector to strengthen disability prevention and rehabilitation. Since the health sector will vary from country to country and also from district to district with regard to the emphasis placed on disability issues, it may be that some districts use only one or two sections of this guide, while others use the entire guide. Some may benefit from the suggestions given here, but may initiate activities differently.

If a district health team has decided to follow the steps in this guide and has formed community and district working groups for DPR, then the team should try to maintain these groups. Each group that contributed to the formulation of action plans could also help to implement and monitor those plans. In addition, these groups would be well prepared to promote collaboration with other sectors involved in rehabilitation.